Tall and Sleek

What Am I?

by Joyce Markovics

Consultant: Eric Darton, Adjunct Faculty
New York University Urban Design and Architecture Studies Program
New York, New York

BEARPORT
PUBLISHING

New York, New York

Credits

Cover, © Felix Lipov/Shutterstock and © Pakhnyushchy/Shutterstock;
2, © FrankvandenBergh/iStock; TOC, © tifonimages/iStock; 4–5, © rimages2007/
Flickr; 6–7, © Antonio Gravante/Dreamstime; 8–9, © anaglic/Shutterstock;
10–11, © Monkey Business Images/Shutterstock; 12–13, © tifonimages/iStock;
14–15, © FrankvandenBergh/iStock and © Arnon Phutthajak/Shutterstock;
16–17, © Clive Sawyer/Alamy; 18–19, © frankysze/iStock; 20–21, © frankysze/iStock;
22–23, © Leonard Zhukovsky/Shutterstock; 24, © T photography/Shutterstock.

Publisher: Kenn Goin
Senior Editor: Joyce Tavolacci
Creative Director: Spencer Brinker
Design: Debrah Kaiser
Photo Researcher: Thomas Persano

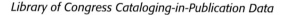

Library of Congress Cataloging-in-Publication Data

Names: Markovics, Joyce L., author.
Title: Tall and sleek : what am I? / by Joyce Markovics.
Description: New York : Bearport Publishing Company, Inc., 2018. | Series:
   American place puzzlers | Includes bibliographical references and index. |
   Identifiers: LCCN 2017039244 (print) | LCCN 2017040290 (ebook) |
ISBN 9781684025374 (ebook) | ISBN 9781684024797 (library)
Subjects: LCSH: Empire State Building (New York, N.Y.)—Juvenile literature.
   | Skyscrapers—New York (State)—New York—Juvenile literature. |
   Manhattan (New York, N.Y.)—Buildings, structures, etc.—Juvenile
   literature. | New York (N.Y.)—Buildings, structures, etc.—Juvenile
   literature.
Classification: LCC F128.8.E46 (ebook) | LCC F128.8.E46 M37 2018 (print) |
   DDC 974.7—dc23
LC record available at https://lccn.loc.gov/2017039244

Contents

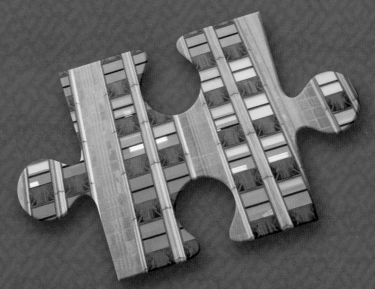

What Am I?

See all of my
windows.

There are
6,514 of them!

I have
73 elevators.

6

They zoom
up and down.

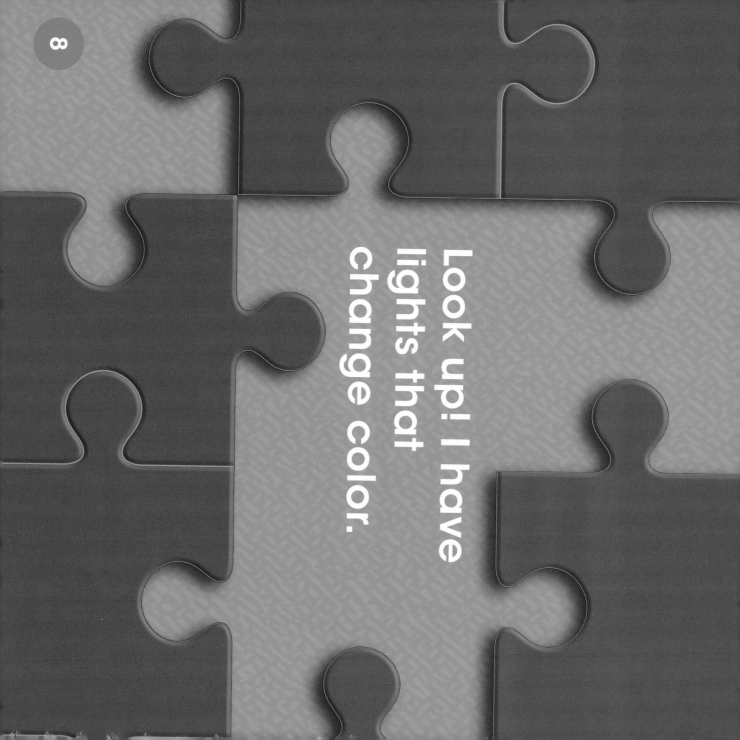

Look up! I have lights that change color.

I am home to
1,000 businesses.

I have
102 floors!

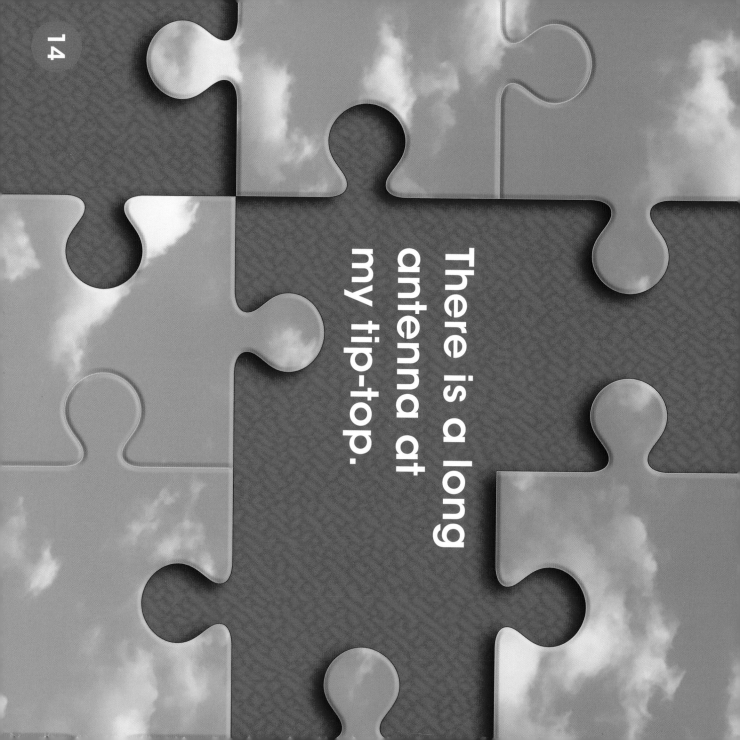

There is a long antenna at my tip-top.

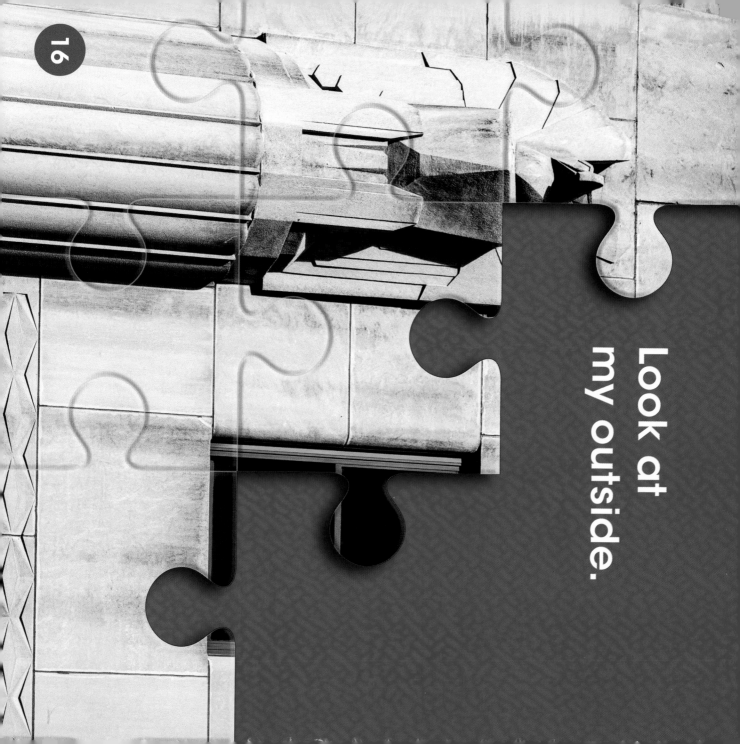

Look at
my outside.

It is covered with sleek, gray stone.

What am I?

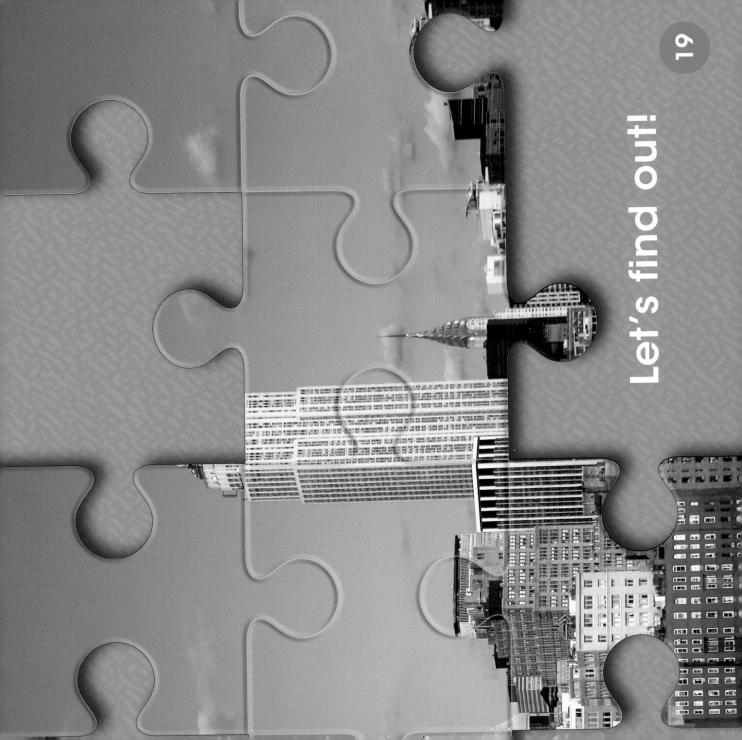

Let's find out!

I am the Empire State Building!

Fast Facts

The Empire State Building is a famous skyscraper. It was built in 1931. For more than 40 years, it was the world's tallest building!

The Empire State Building

Total Height:	1,454 feet (443 m), including the antenna
Weight:	365,000 tons (331,122 mt)
Number of Floors:	102
Amount of Office Space:	2.8 million square feet (260,129 sq. m)
Number of Light Bulbs:	3,194,547
Cool Fact:	About 10,000 people visit the Empire State Building each day!

Where Am I?

The Empire State Building is located on Fifth Avenue in New York City.

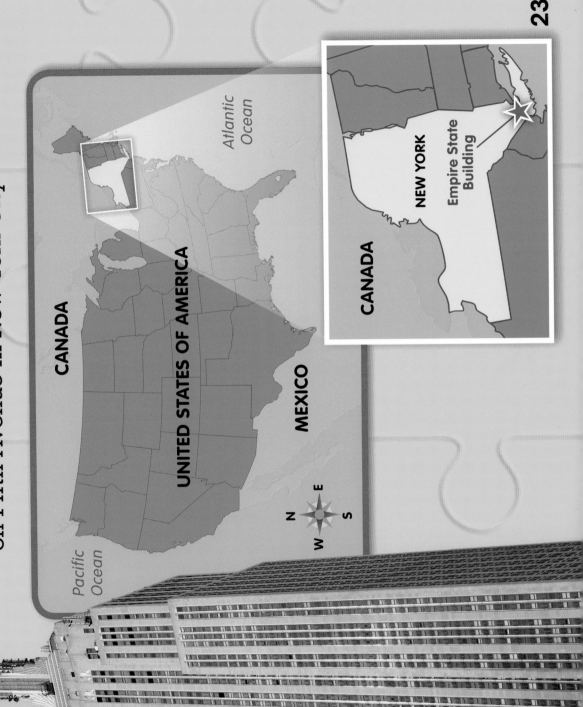

Pacific
Ocean

CANADA

UNITED STATES OF AMERICA

MEXICO

Atlantic
Ocean

N
W E
S

CANADA

NEW YORK

Empire State
Building

Index

Read More

Bullard, Lisa. *The Empire State Building.* Minneapolis, MN: Lerner (2010).

Mansfield, Andy. *Pop-Up New York.* New York: Lonely Planet Kids (2016).

Learn More Online

To learn more about the Empire State Building, visit
www.bearportpublishing.com/AmericanPlacePuzzlers

About the Author

Joyce Markovics is a proud New Yorker who lives in a very old house along the Hudson River. Every morning, she admires the Empire State Building on her way to work.